A Heart's Journey

Poems of
Change, Wonder, and Reflection

by Brooke Cullen

A Heart's Journey

Poems of
Change, Wonder, and Reflection

by Brooke Cullen

Railroad Street Press
394 Railroad Street, Suite 2
St. Johnsbury, VT 05819

Published in the United States by Railroad Street Press, St. Johnsbury, Vermont.

ISBN: 9780984473878

Library of Congress Control Number 2010931426
   1.   Poetry

Jacket design by Susanna V. Walden.
Illustrations by Paul Samuel Doerfler.

First Edition 2010

Railroad Street Press
394 Railroad Street, Suite 2
St. Johnsbury, VT 05819
(802) 748-3551
www.railroadstreetpress.com

About the Author

I was born in Dayton, Ohio in the 1950's. When I was nine, my parents moved us from Dayton to Scott County in Southwestern Virginia where they had their original roots. I had no idea at that time how that rural, mountainous region with its scenic hills and valleys and dynamic history would impact my life.

After the move, we stayed a year in the town of Gate City, where my maternal grandparents lived. Gate City, so named, by its place of standing near the gap of two mountains and the gateway to the coalfields of Virginia, Kentucky, and West Virginia. Both of my grandfathers had in fact, worked for the coal mines as builders.

Scott County is home to two rivers, the Holston and the Clinch. This area was once part of the Shawnee and Cherokee hunting grounds. It was a dangerous section of the western frontier from the 1750's until the mid 1790's because of the hostilities with the Indians. However, early settlers still moved in along these rivers to build their homesteads and partake of the fertile farming soil and abundant wildlife.

In 1769 Daniel Boone and friend, James Findley, along with several other men were the first to come into the area to blaze trails through this wilderness. Daniel Boone and his wife even settled in the vicinity for a time on a Clinch River settlement. Then Boone talked Captain Russell into going to Kentucky to form a settlement. But, after the killing of both of their young sons on Powell Mountain by the Shawnee in October 1773, Boone would stay put on the Clinch until 1775 when he again left and successfully founded Boonesboro, Kentucky.

Several of my ancestors including the Moores, Poages, Duncans, and Smiths helped settle this territory despite the many Indian raids and uprisings. Other frontier families including the Pattons, Ingles, Drapers, and Harmons were either killed or captured and my ancestors were no exception.

Gate City (formerly called Estilville) with a population of around 2,000 is bordered by the Allegheny Mountains and by parts of the Clinch and Powell Mountain ridges. After a full year in Gate City, my Dad moved us to a small simple house 15 miles away in the town of Hiltons, to a place called, "Poor Valley", with a population of around 300 people. This is the same area where the Carter musical family was born and raised. AP Carter, famed as the "father of country music", was the Uncle of June Carter Cash. AP Carter and his wife, Sara Doughtery Carter, his sister in law, Maybelle Addington Carter (June's Mother) formed a trio and held performances there as far back as the 1930's.

The Holston River was a few miles from our home and I went there on many occasions either to fish or wade near Lunsford Dam. When I was 19 years old I moved out on my own, and a year later out of the state taking the home grown values I learned and discovered with me. That same spirit of life and folklore gave me a love for reading and history. Literature and poetry became more than just pastimes, they became my passions.

I have lived in Vermont's Northeast Kingdom for the last twenty years and have formed a very strong bond with the region, similar to my kinship with Virginia. One thing which has always been very clear to me is that the value of our lives shouldn't be taken for granted. Our past, our hopes and dreams for the future are what make us who we are and there are many physical and mental experiences waiting for us to enjoy.

Although I finished my first personal journal by the time I graduated high school, writing would have to take a backseat to my busy life of being a wife and mother and later to working and running a business. Finally, when my Dad was dying of cancer in 2003, I picked up a second journal of poetry I had started 3 years earlier, and began writing again. This time determined to finish it in my spare time and to research and catalog my Father's ancestral roots.

Little did I know, it would take five years to complete the later project. The work I was doing gave me courage not only to accept my Father's death, but to accept other hardships I was experiencing. Only now can I honestly say that if you have a dream, you should go after it. For no matter your age or experiences, dreams really can come true! Thanks be to God.

I would like to express my sincere love and gratitude to Paul Doerfler, for his belief in me and for the use of his wonderful paintings that he so graciously allowed me to use in this book.

SEASONS

Seasons in Time

Each season in time, has a special quality to cherish I find.
Slow long days of summer offer an added fun, as I spy the
strangest winged creatures at play.
Evening tree frogs take over the singing for the songbirds
of the day.
With boisterous sounds they drown out the tireless crickets
with their say.
And I give in to the urge to go barefoot through thick green
clover, after it's cooled in the smallest of shade.
When autumn comes I, dearly, miss smelling fresh cut grass
and indulging in a tall glass of Mom's homemade lemonade.

Yet, remembering the weeks of heat from a sizzling, hot July.
sun, I embrace the benefits of fall's sudden return.
Those colorful woods encourage each walk to lengthen into
a full-fledged hike.
And old sugar maple trees are a sight to behold with burning
reds that bleed against the delicate blues of a defenseless sky.
Then later, I'm beaming with delight when a snowy frost
appears to glitter with a shimmering white.

And later the forests hibernate in blankets of deep snow

that light up the black seductive nights.

So, don't take my seasons for each I would miss.

And how low my spirit would be without their wonderful gifts!

Meadows of May

In search of the many greens of May to the top of the highest
hill I must go.

The worn trail is clear of any late spring snow.

My fast pace wanes to enjoy robust smells and intimate views
into spacious rich pastures and overgrown forgotten fields.

I hear and see some mallard ducks dunking in a shallow river
by an abandoned farm's stone mill.

And clumps of graceful willow branches drape and sway in soft
breezes of a prevailing north wind.

Tall meadow flowers greet me as they wave and politely bend.

But, the richest colored blooms dwell in narrow valley
crevices, where pods live among mossy, aged craggy rocks.

Bashfully shy, they hide their painted faces, and my eyes are wide
in the fullest of gazes.

Miniature indigo violets and romantic tiny bells of an aquatic
sea blue, peep out along the way as I drench my soul in a hundred
different hues.

Summer's Evening

The last fragment of light frantically dances across the lavish
land where grassy hills stand watch over succulent mountain
valleys.
Then as evening is nye, a lone catbird sings a series of countless
festive tunes quite professionally.
A perfect summer day ends and from my yard's view I, soberly,
watch slumber time come.
Fat evening moths arrive to fly with the last few butterflies
 that are seeking a sheltered nights home.
Fundamental changes take place to complete the shadowy scene,
and like always I feel I'm receiving a most special treat.

June's Enchantment

Behold summer's June that enchants my sleepy flower
garden, into life once again.

Whimsical minute hummingbirds return to become friends
for a short while, and I turn merry with a permanent smile.

Streaming tangles of thick, speckled ivy give pretty ladybugs
a temporary home, and to others who will eventually come.

Round marbled stones I placed many seasons ago curve the
path on the brown pebbles below.

And blooming flower buds compete in an early,
yet, dazzling fashion show.

My nearby lily pond adds a floating mist to the sultry air
and I revel in its redeeming sight.

And my heart truly believes nature spirits are scurrying
about in this charming garden of mine!

Rose Cottage

Across the eastern cool waters of the Northern Atlantic there
stands an old-world summer cottage on English ground.
Not far from a rural village it sits on a pasture's hill where the finest
grazing sheep and wild pink roses abound.
Red sentries of heavy ivy vines studied me at the entrance iron
gate and an orange brick walk led me to her wrap around porch
shaded by healthy beech and walnut trees.
Fed by her maternal stature, one can't help but, be spellbound
within her private borders.
Elongated, double paned windows allow the light to play upon her
shiny metallic ceilings.
Century old fixtures and a masterful, walk-in rock fireplace bring
fantasy to life, reminiscent of the forest witch's house in
Hansel and Gretel.
Each scrolled, red mahogany doorway is rooted in gray stone floors
which are decorated with mosaic drawings that take you into a
visual dream.
And while on her back veranda, you're at peace with views of a
butterfly filled, floral garden complete with a gurgling, wide stream.
In the distance, you'll often hear a traveling train's sharp,
resounding whistle.
And during the days of early spring, the locals tell of strange

winds which blow across her knoll that mimic a lead wolf calling for his pack before the sound dies to a gentle whisper.

Yet, I haven't been able to revisit her, that one brief summer's encounter with "Rose Cottage" was enough to allow me the right to love her.

Brooke Cullen

The Butterfly Dance

Drenched in morning sunlight, she woke from her night.

Then she spread her graceful, exquisite wings.

Across the hills, she heard the babbling brook sing.

And directly below, her enchanting meadow home glowed.

In warmth from the sun's rays of an ancient gold, she no longer shivered from the fretful cold.

The spring wild flowers were awake and patiently waiting.

But, she slowly drifted along daydreaming.

Then she approached the first tender bloom, as if it was her wedded groom.

Yet, when she kissed its dew, she bowed and flew.

Speeding off to another, she paused to drink and it was even sweeter.

Clinging to each petal briefly, breathing peacefully, she performed her ballet again, so beautifully.

Romance of the Firefly

Actually you're not a fly at all, though that's your name of call.

Ever since I met your clever kind, you captivate my curious mind.

I'd like to know how you control that blinking light.

And when I see you in the early evening sky, I realize what

a special creature you are, firefly.

And I must tell you, watching your nightly glows, has really

 helped me forget my worst woes.

Though I can't wait for your return each year, I've noticed your

family's getting sparser, my dear.

So next time you see me, believe me when I say, "I adore you",

and spread the word to all your lovely species.

The Annual Cricket Concert

The biggest crickets are resting meekly under the umbrella of the
rotting boat dock.
Later they'll perform in an outdoor concert beginning at eight
o'clock.
And a family of native ducks, has reserved special sitting for their
entire flock.
The pond's bullfrogs say they'll attend, but only if it's over by ten.
And whatever the weather, a mixed medley will be sung at the end.
Those cranky crows won't be a problem, for they've agreed to nest
around the next bend.

It's sure to be a spectacular event, after all, the visiting bats
have an air show and it won't cost a cent.
I heard the lightening bugs were taken off the menu, for they're
providing extra lights for a better view.
And no one needs a ticket, or, so say those hundreds of talented
crickets.

Favorite Summer Pleasures

Sitting under white pillow towers of cumulus clouds in baby
blue skies,

smelling wildflowers till you feel a little high,

standing on a water's shoreline admiring crafty seabirds while they
socialize and fly,

laughing so hard that you cry,

walking barefoot on a beach's wet sand,

and holding your lover's hand,

hearing finches sing to the early light,

wishing on shooting stars as their tails glow and glide against the
backdrop of a hollow night,

finding galaxies in a canopy of a billion stars,

picnicking under a shady tree in a natural park,

and growing love within your heart.

October Geese

On a crisp morning in mid October, I went for a brisk stroll to visit impressive Joe pies and goldenrods and yellow dry lakes of hay fields near a backwoods forest.

Squawking blue jays in some dispute soon interrupted the abundant silence.

Much likened to an amateur singing out of key in a Broadway chorus, the intrusion was quickly excused and I continued to reap the benefits of the sensual surroundings.

A little later, a lesser commotion commenced when remote sounds getting closer struck a memory from late spring.

Old friends, the Canadian Geese, were on their departed seasonal flight.

Poised in a trance, my eyes focused to capture tiny black images climbing to great height.

Seeing those sassy rear spotters return young stragglers back into formation intrigued me.

Yet, the surging energy I embraced, quickly, eroded and I became limb and at ease.

The heaviness of my weight returned when they, elusively, faded from my failing sight.

And I yelled out to them, "Godspeed", with all of my might!

Snow Prayer

Winter come home with your fresh fallen snow, and bring
back those alpine views I love and know.

Dress up each pine with white caps so fancy, that each little
branch bends low in plenty.

Make your winds blow in a wispy light way, that snow clouds erupt
throughout my day.

Give grace back to the lonely, grieving land with rich, frosty deep
snow, where sleighs can glide and easily go.

Bless me with your ornaments in a gleeful way.

So, I'll remember my youth when big snows brought a full day of
heavenly play.

A Walk Through Barren Trees

January's inhospitable blasts of hellish winds, rather unbearable this month I find.

A full day of warmth seems like a long forgotten face, for everything is severely frozen in place.

And winter has my hardwood trees so barren, that distant hills are speechless and solemn.

Yet, just ahead, I hear cascading waters from a half-frozen creek, and see thriving winter birds as they spy me from their crystallized evergreen peeks.

Last night's powerful storm has left a lingering, naughty howling.

But, there's an occasional faint whimper that's almost inviting.

Just like a smitten lover questions and wonders, how long will it be till he gets over her?

Then, sadly, admits in his heart maybe never.

I'm reminded that winter possesses mysteries, which bring both delight and great misery.

Ode to Old Man Winter

Old bitter winter, how harsh can be, that Nor'easters and Gales we often see.

Blizzards arrive to catch many off guard, having no mercy for men caught in the grip of their glory.

And Jack Frost freezes all to ice without a thought of feeling sorry.

Trees in the deep woods must endure those formidable destructive winds, and offer shelter to many furry and feathered friends.

Though provocative starry nights and a huge hunter's moon are unforgettable, let us remember, "Old Man Winter" has a reputation for a daring long reign.

Until Mother Nature allows the return of Miss Spring, may we be vigil, and give some respect to this mighty Snow King.

Winter's Reason

Winter is not graced by the company of a dependable strong
sun.

And darkness brings nightfall before the afternoon hours have had
their proper run.

There aren't any Robins or Cardinals left in the yard to welcome
a new day, and bursting sunsets fade too quickly away.

Every creature possesses a wanton hunger for food and rest,
and even the grass was long put to bed.

A strange stillness comes to comfort yet, leaves behind an annoying
unknown ring.

And our minds and hands often crave to complete some project or
unfinished thing.

 Possibly, there's a rebirth living in winter's reason.

If we got better acquainted with winter, maybe, we'd acquire a
philosophical bond with this baffling final season.

KINDRED PLACES

A Poet's World

Grandma's House

Country Farm

Wonderland

Sahara

Ocean Yearning

Resting Place

Mysterious Moon

The Milky Way

Cushendon Bay

Yesterday

Twilight Time

A Place Called Camelot

Age of Lullabies

My Days in Heather

A Poet's World

Poets speak of untold passion and broken dreams, of what is
and what was once deemed.
With tired hands they perilously write of burning love that
tragically crumbles.
Far into the anatomies of a multitude of restless nights, they create
an oasis of melodies or never ending prolific struggles.
Caught between war and peace, they calm the hand so it may hear
the willing soul that channels the voices into words and people.
What they write becomes no more or less of what life and fate
allows.

At times those unexplainable transmissions abruptly end, only to
be later reconstructed by unknown forces that scream and bellow.
Though some rhymes may forever stand in a morbid place
drenched in sorrow.
Others shall become healing miracles, such as a blind man who
walks from darkness into a world of sight or a deaf who wakes with
ears that hear.
So, abides such revelations hiding in beloved poems
waiting to be freed by readers, who will remember them quite dear.

Grandma's House

Cozy, old clapboard house in my past, may I tell you, you went away much too fast?

And now, how sad, you're far beyond my reach.

Yet, I kept the love that grew within your sturdy walls and the lessons you still teach.

I hear distant laughter and young children's chatter, from a time free of bothersome matters.

So, surely, there must be some of my decaying echoes that remain in your special places I once wondered.

And may I ask, do your cracked sidewalks display any leftover marks from the many hopscotch games I hurriedly scratched?

And how, I'd like to speak to the little wadding brook, whose clear waters used to flow nearby, to see if there's a coin or two left behind from all the pennies I pitched in to make secret wishes come true.

Though Grandma and Paw have long passed on, I want to say, there's no way I'll ever forget about you!

Brooke Cullen

Country Farm

Father time take me back to the country home I once had, for there my life was innocent and new.

I won't complain about the tedious farm chores and that's the gospel truth.

After dark, I'll quietly rest on the porch with Pa and look for those elusive, bright shooting stars.

I promise each time I get a brand new penny; it'll be put in Ma's old chipped mason jar.

And when that rainy day comes, I'll gladly spend it on something she really needs.

Milking cows, bailing hay, or sewing seeds, won't be a problem at all, if on Sundays I'll be allowed to climb that big, gnarly oak tree.

And even though, there aren't any stores, or malls, or movie theaters close by, I'll never mention it or even ask why.

Wonderland

Eyes of a child stay with me in wonder, and help me grow ever
fonder.

So, soothing blue skies will remain a safe haven, and I won't be
afraid to go to Heaven.

So, each reflection of light from the sun's brilliance will continue
to be seen as a shiny piece of treasure.

And the crescent moon's silvery glow admired like a gift that's
humbly cherished.

So, euphoric rainbows in the endless vast sky, fill my heart with
joyous music where it lives to be replayed till the very day I wilt
and die.

Sahara

A dry wind blew across the Sahara sands, whirling little specks
of her golden grit above the land.
Masquerading as ghostly shadows against the setting hot sun,
they played about as children do in fun.
Yet, quickly, died as silently as they had appeared, to be forgotten
by the arid landscape where they had formed.
The day's unbearable heat began to slowly retreat, and the sky
turned a jubilant red purple before the first star's feet.
Then darkness fell upon Sahara's face allowing the cool air to
tenderly kiss her to sleep.

Brooke Cullen

Ocean Yearning

Rolling seas of northern Maine how I miss your roaring sounds, which moved in timeless waves across countless rocks and parcels of grassy dunes that dressed the bare sandy grounds.

Your cooling abundant splashes that caressed my tired naked feet, as I walked on your warm summer beach was a soothing welcomed relief.

I wish I still stood near your sun, mirrored waters when they flashed a thousand sparkling signals and molded them into blinding light ships that I christened, "The Diamond Fleet".

Your refreshing predictable breezes that tasseled each strand of my hair are whining in my ears, like a pair of empathetic seagulls sulking after they end a day of frolicking play.

I often think of that lingering peace, you brought from somewhere far away.

While collecting little alabaster shells, I saw your crawling tide recede and heard echoing clangs from the metal buoys bobbing about in your busy bay.

The smiles I wore then were of a different kind, ones that remained like a lovely mask that kept sadness from seeping in and told nagging thoughts to silence their say.

Resting Place

A pine wooden lock chest, is where my family treasures lay at rest.
Cut strands of baby curls, and faded photos of both boys and girls
are neatly sorted and stored in old used envelopes.

Grandpa's love letters from the 1930's are bundled with satin red
ribbons, and tucked inside a deep pocket of one of Grandma's
ruffled handmade aprons.

A shiny, round gold locket my Mom wore, and fancy veiled hats
she once adored, rest among her white cotton gowns tinged with
age.

Great-Grandma's oval cameo brooch is pinned to a silk black
pouch filled with lavender and sage.

And Aunt Hattie's well assembled and useful crazy quilt has a
proper nesting place at the very bottom.

Though occasionally displayed during the Holidays, its revered year
round like all of my priceless heirlooms.

Lastly, my Dad's favorite, cardboard cigar box holds Uncle Willie's
glass colored marbles and a fine set of jacks.

What more could anyone ever want, I ask?

Mysterious Moon

That man in the moon has thousands of memories but, he'll never share just one of his stories.

Often with a Cheshire cat grin, he changes like a seasoned acrobat into the oddest shapes.

And quite the illusionist, he can disappear in the most amazing escapes.

Some say his bewildering fires, can fill one with the wildest desires.

Yet, many know he emits this unique, universal peace, that puts most men's hearts at ease.

I've seen him look virtually bestial, then turn undeniably jolly.

And ancient civilizations considered him to be rather holy.

Though he won't tell me why, I've never really seen him cry.

No one will argue that he's more of a friend than a foe.

And if he didn't exist, I'm positive that night sky and those neighboring stars would seem lost and desperately alone.

The Milky Way

White stars, yellow, blue, and red stars, how I have admired you
from afar.
And there are so many of you, just remembering your names is a
challenge for even those studious bright scholars.
And what a pleasing exhibit you maintain for my eyes to encounter,
that it is hardly worth comparing to any other.
Of all the adventures in my life your twinkling, gallery of
compelling lights, has always been my most beloved sight.
And I can't help but ponder if you lie near some heavenly portal,
where man can't go until he earns the right to be immortal.

Brooke Cullen

Cushendon Bay

Oh Cushendon Bay, your waters bring life to thirsty, jagged cliffs
that thrust their forms against your barren breast.
And all the nearby gulls cry out your name before they seek their
needed rest.
You may belong to the living by day.
Yet, by night those souls lost within you take ownership and begin
an ominous play.
And under the cloak of darkness, I hear such turbulent and violent
sprays.

But, I sense there is some comfort in your prestigious vessel so
deep.
For just before dawn, the water settles to a rocking cradle peace,
that must, eventually, put them back to sleep.

Yesterday

The fun of taffy pulling, no one bothers doing.

That Buster Brown suit, long replaced by hooded jackets were oh,

so cute.

Those stylish, attractive brimmed hats, I never see for men now

wear little caps.

Once ladies were in hi-fashion in those fancy twelve button shoes,

but you won't find one left on any store shelf to view.

You probably won't ever read by an oil lamps flickering glow,

either, for they're an old relic, too.

I don't understand why good things have to go away, do you?

Twilight Time

The passive sun sets low in the far western sky having reached midway across the living planet's formation.

Vibrant, translucent light beams cross the horizon then sink in complete exhaustion.

In a magnificent colorful explosion, the burning orange sun says goodbye to the endless benevolent heavens.

Yet, clings to those last few trickling moments in such a passionate dying performance, that a growing sense of vulnerability causes my heart to yearn.

And if my eyes spill a single tear, my body's stinging with a blistering torrid burn.

A Place Called Camelot

When I was becoming of age, I memorized a tale found in a
storybook's page.

Believing in the myths and legends I read in my younger years,
and waiting for a handsome, brave Prince to come and dry my
mournful tears.

Boldly, telling inferior others, I belonged to another.

Dreaming of his first kiss, I longed to live in the romance of
Camelot's bliss.

Yet, strangely, he's passed me by, or maybe, he couldn't come for
he had died.

Now that I'm much older I'm wondering if I got it all wrong, and if
Camelot only exists in that song.

I suppose lonely hearts should keep hoping, but, frankly, I've
stopped looking.

Age of Lullabies

A soft hush that whispered in my ear so dearly, has gone away completely.

The nursery rhymes, I knew by heart, are an obscured memory that dwells in the dark.

My aging arms and legs have become more rigid and increasingly feeble, and, lately, I don't see as many people.

The Sandman rarely visits either, although, he used to be a most reliable and devoted friend.

And Mother's daily readings from little picture books have long ago ended.

So much goodness and tenderness lives in my past, and I'm longing for a lullaby if only I could ask.

Brooke Cullen

My Days in Heather

Rolling hills of Emerald Isle, how I miss them still!

Clouds of milky mist settled low to build in sleepy valleys till they
would fill.

Those frequent dainty rains were blessed sights, for they made
the grass grow tall and lush during the summer's warm and humid
nights.

As a bonny youth in County Claire, I romped and played in
picturesque fertile fields and breathed the freshest highland air.

Memories of gathering pink and purple heather in full bloom glory,
make my heartbeats pound with such speed and trembling fury.

And I hear those wailing wild Irish winds so vividly alive, that they
hauntingly chant, "Where are you my child?"

Yet, I'm not there today, "Dear Old Ireland", forever will hold
a piece of my heart within her loving hands.

About the Illustrator

Paul Samuel Doerfler was born and raised in Weehawken, New Jersey, just across the Hudson River from the Empire State Building. He attended The Boston Museum School of Fine Arts, where he was a painting major for three years under a Ford Fellowship from 1966 to 1969. While still in high school in Weehawken, he attended the Arts Student's League in New York City. The collection of landscapes used in this book were painted in 2003 and 2004 while Paul was a resident of Quebec, Canada. Paul's early inspiration came from the impressionists Monet, Cezanne, and Van Gogh. When painting, Paul focuses on light, space, and time. He now resides in St. Johnsbury, Vermont.

www.ingramcontent.com/pod-product-compliance
Lightning Source LLC
LaVergne TN
LVHW010016070426
835511LV00001B/6